# *Where Is Jesus?*

Matthew 27:62–66; 28:1–9

(Easter)

## by Mary Manz Simon
## Illustrated by Dennis Jones

SAINT LOUIS

**Books by Mary Manz Simon from Concordia Publishing House**

## Hear Me Read Level 1 Series
What Next?
Drip Drop
Jibber Jabber
Hide the Baby
Toot! Toot!
Bing!
Whoops!
Send a Baby
A Silent Night
Follow That Star
Row the Boat
Rumble, Rumble
Who Will Help?
Sit Down
Come to Jesus
Too Tall, Too Small
Hurry, Hurry!
Where Is Jesus?

## Hear Me Read Big Book Series
Drip Drop
Who Will Help?
Sit Down
Where Is Jesus?

## Hear Me Read Level 2 Series
The No-Go King
Hurray for the Lord's Army
The Hide-and-Seek Prince
Daniel and the Tattletales
The First Christmas
Through the Roof
A Walk on the Waves
Thank You, Jesus

## Little Visits ® Series
Little Visits on the Go
Little Visits for Toddlers
Little Visits with Jesus
Little Visits Every Day

Stop! It's Christmas
God's Children Pray
My First Diary

4  5  6  7  8  9  10      00  99  98

_____

Name

_____

Date

Presented by

_____

**To the Adult:**

Early readers need two kinds of reading. They need to be read to, and they need to do their own reading. The Hear Me Read Bible Stories series helps you to encourage your child with both kinds.

For example, your child might read this book as you sit together. Listen attentively. Assist gently, if needed. Encourage, be patient, and be very positive about your child's efforts.

Then perhaps you'd like to share the selected Bible story in an easy-to-understand translation or paraphrase.

Using both types of reading gives your child a chance to develop new skills and pride in reading. You share and support your child's excitement.

As a mother and a teacher, I anticipate the joy your child will feel in saying, "Hear me read Bible stories!"

*Mary Manz Simon*

**To Hank**
*Psalm 128*

"Jesus is not alive.

Jesus is in the tomb."

"Jesus said, 'I will rise.'"

"People will say,

'Where is Jesus?' "

"Go!

Shut the tomb."

"Roll, roll the stone."

"Roll the stone here."

The tomb is shut.

"I am not afraid.

The tomb is shut.

People will not say,

'Where is Jesus?' "

"I am not afraid.

Jesus is not alive.

Jesus is in the tomb."

The stone!

The stone!

"Do not be afraid."

"Where is Jesus?"

"Jesus said, 'I will rise.'
Jesus is not here."

"Jesus is alive."

"Go.

Say, 'Jesus is alive!' "

Jesus is alive!

## About the Author

Mary Manz Simon holds a doctoral degree in education with a specialty in early childhood education. She has taught at levels from preschool through postgraduate. Dr. Simon is the bestselling author of more than 30 children's books, including *Little Visits with Jesus*. She and her husband, the Reverend Henry A. Simon, are the parents of three children.